CREATIVE CHRISTMAS CRAFTS

This book is dedicated to **LENA** and **ALL KIDS**

THIS BOOK BELONGS TO:

....

First published in Sweden by Bonnier Carlsen Bokförlag, Stockholm, Sweden, 2016 as *Kreativa Karins jul för barn!*

First English edition published by Sky Pony Press, 2018.

Sky Pony Press books may be purchased in bulk at special discounts for sales promotion, corporate gifts, fund-raising, or educational purposes. Special editions can also be created to specifications. For details, contact the Special Sales Department, Sky Pony Press, 307 West 36th Street, 11th Floor, New York, NY 10018 or info@skyhorsepublishing.com.

Sky Pony® is a registered trademark of Skyhorse Publishing, Inc.®, a Delaware corporation.

Visit our website at www.skyponypress.com.

10 9 8 7 6 5 4 3 2 1

Manufactured in China, 2022.
This product conforms to CPSIA 2008

Library of Congress Cataloging-in-Publication Data is available on file.

Graphic design: Karin Andersson
Photography: Katja Ragnstam

Paperback ISBN: 978-1-5107-7094-2
Hardcover ISBN: 978-1-5107-3275-9

Karin Andersson

CREATIVE CHRISTMAS CRAFTS

25+ HOLIDAY ACTIVITIES FOR FAMILIES

Sky Pony Press
New York, NY

GOOD TO HAVE ON HAND

BRUSHES

FUSE BEAD PEGBOARD

HOLE PUNCH

GLUE GUN

SCISSORS

PERMANENT MARKERS IN MULTIPLE COLORS

uni POSCA

LIQUID GLUE

GLUE STICK

IRON

DOUBLE-SIDED TAPE

WASHI TAPE

CONTENTS

MERRY CHRISTMAS!

Cool
CHRISTMAS CARDS

YOU'LL NEED:
Construction/cardstock paper
Lightweight paper
Scissors
Glue

Who doesn't love getting a **CHRISTMAS CARD** in the mail? Just grab some paper and glue and you can make great cards in a flash!

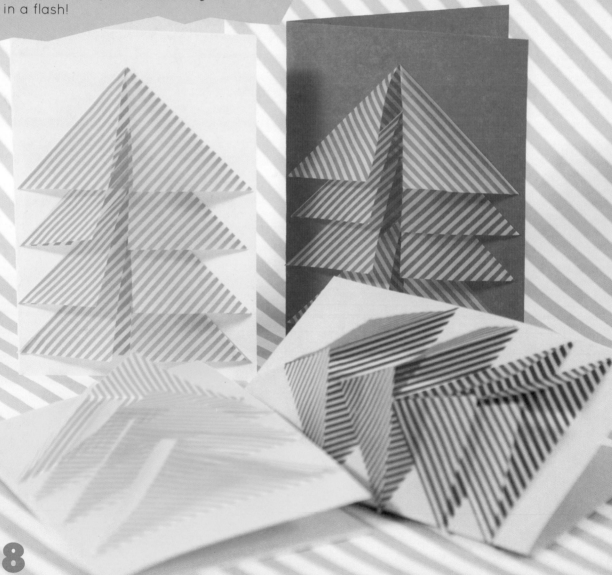

1 Take a sheet of thick, 8 ½ x 11 inch paper, and two square sheets of light-weight paper.

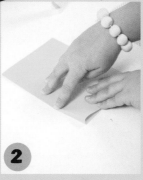

2 Fold the thick paper in half. This will be the card itself.

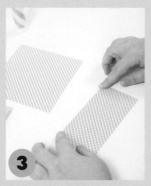

3 Fold the square sheets of thinner paper in half.

4 Unfold the square light-weight sheets of paper, and cut them along the folded line with the scissors.

5 Take one piece of thinner paper, and fold one corner from the short side down to the edge of one long side.

6 Fold the opposite corner in the same way so you get a triangle.

7 Fold all your pieces of thin paper the same way so you have four triangles.

8 Take one of the triangles and spread glue on the back of it.

9 Stick the triangle to the top of the card.

10 Fold up the flaps of the triangle and stick the next triangle underneath the flaps.

11 Glue the other triangles the same way until you have a tree. This Christmas card is ready!

Cool crafting!

Send **ANIMAL HUG CARDS** to someone you like!

To Santa Claus

Merry Christmas Grandma

HUG CARD

HOW YOU DO IT

1. Get a sheet of 8 ½ x 11 inch size cardstock paper, and fold in the top and bottom sides, folding so one side overlaps the other just a little. That way it looks like the arms are hugging when you fold them.

2. Draw a head and wings or arms, and cut out the card with a pair of scissors.

3. Draw the eyes with a permanent marker.

4. Cut out a nose using some glitter paper or other pretty paper, and glue it onto the card. Write a greeting on the animal's tummy and send the card to someone special.

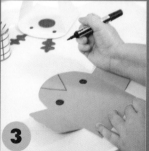

10

YOU'LL NEED:

Cardstock paper
Glitter paper
(or other pretty paper)

Glue
Permanent markers
Scissors

CHRISTMAS TREE CARDS

HOW YOU DO IT

1. Grab a sheet of cardstock paper. Cut out a star in glitter paper or other pretty paper. Glue the star at the top of the card.

2. Glue two drinking straws next to each other, under the star and down to the bottom of the card. Snip off the straws off at the bottom of the card.

3. Glue a short piece of a drinking straw right under the star, and then another, slightly longer piece of straw under the first, short one.

4. Keep adding longer and longer pieces of drinking straws until it looks like a Christmas tree. It's ready to go!

YOU'LL NEED:

Thick paper, like cardstock
Glitter paper (or other pretty paper)

Plastic drinking straws
Glue
Scissors

All you need to create great **CHRISTMAS TREE CARDS** is a few plastic drinking straws, glue, and some nice-looking paper.

COOL CHRISTMAS CARDS

Awesome
CHRISTMAS GIFTS

The very best **CHRISTMAS GIFTS** you can give are those you've made yourself—they're not only fun to make, they're great to receive!

PEARL BOXES!

YOU'LL NEED:

Plastic fuse beads
Fuse bead pegboard
Iron
Parchment paper
Glue
Big wooden bead, button, or pretty pearl

1 Start by building the sides of the box on the pegboard. You'll need four square pieces and two rectangular pieces (they'll be the same height as the squares, but two rows narrower).

2 Fuse the fuse beads with an iron. Set some parchment paper on top of the pearls and iron them until the fuse beads lie very flat. Ask a grown-up to help you if you've never used an iron before.

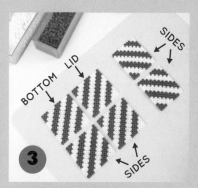

3 Now you have four sides (two square sides and two narrow sides), a bottom, and a lid.

4 It's time to glue the box together. Pick up one of the squares and apply glue all along one edge.

5 Place the glued edge against another, identical square piece. Now you have the bottom of the box.

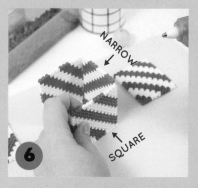

6 Glue the other sides of the box. The square sides are glued opposite each other, and the narrow sides are glued opposite each other.

7 You'll use the last square as your lid. Glue a fuse bead in each corner, a little bit in from the edge, so the lid sits nicely on the box.

8 Glue a nice button or pearl on top of the lid so it's easy to open and close the box.

9 Now the box is made, and is ready to be filled with something fun!

AWESOME CHRISTMAS GIFTS

KNICKKNACK JARS!

Recycle old glass jars and fill them with fuse-bead characters and glittering snow. The perfect **CHRISTMAS GIFT** is almost ready!

ALL KIDS ARE GOOD KIDS!

YOU'LL NEED:

Glass jars
Fuse beads
Fuse bead pegboard
Iron
Parchment paper
Glue
Sugar

1 Start by building a fuse-bead character on the bead pegboard. Make sure that it fits inside the glass jar.

2 Set a sheet of parchment paper between the fuse beads and the iron, and iron the beads flat. Ask a grown-up to help you if you've never used an iron before.

3 Attach the fuse-bead character to the inside of the jar's lid with some glue. Let the glue set for a little bit.

4 Pour the sugar, or some other snowlike matter you have at home, into the jar.

5 Place the fuse-bead character upside down into the jar.

6 Screw on the lid.

7 Turn the jar upside down so the snow falls and covers the inside of the jar's lid.

TIP!

If you don't have any sugar handy, it will look just as nice if you use grated coconut or pieces of cotton for snow at the bottom of the jar.

AWESOME CHRISTMAS GIFTS

OWL BIRD FEEDERS

YOU'LL NEED:

Milk carton
Glue
Scissors
Hobby paint
Brush and Q-tips
Long needle
Thick string
Birdseed
Wooden skewer

16

1

Glue the opening of the milk carton shut.

2

Paint the milk carton with white hobby paint—this will make the other paint stick much better later. Let the paint dry.

3

Draw a wing on each side of the carton, and an opening on what will be the owl's belly.

4

Using a pair of small scissors, carefully cut out the wings, and the opening for the belly.

5

Paint the entire carton in any color you like.

6

Make dots on the owl with a Q-tip—using a cotton tip makes it much easier to make fine, round dots.

7

Paint the eyes on with a Q-tip and use a brush for the beak.

8

The owl is almost ready! To hang it, you'll need some string at the very top.

9

Thread a long needle with some thick string, and push it through the glued opening at the top.

10

Make a perch for the bird by pushing a wooden skewer straight through the carton, front to back.

11

Fill the owl with birdseed or some other yummy treat that birds like.

12

The owl is ready to hang, or to be wrapped up as a Christmas gift! (If you do this, put the seeds in a bag with the feeder.)

AWESOME CHRISTMAS GIFTS

Great
GIFT WRAPPERS

Oh, **CREATIVE GIFT PACKAGES** are so exciting! Wrap gifts up in your own, personally designed and painted Christmas wrapping paper, or make pretty animal boxes with ears and noses made with glitter paper!

YOUR OWN CHRISTMAS WRAPPING PAPER

HOW YOU DO IT

1 Cut one sheet of solid-color gift wrapping paper.

2 Use a brush and different colors to paint a nice design on the paper.

3 Let the paper dry for a bit before you wrap your gift.

4 Tie a nice ribbon around the package, and the Christmas gift is done!

TIP! Using your pegboard and fuse beads, make small Santas, snowmen, reindeer, Christmas trees, or packages, and glue them to pieces of thick cardstock. Punch a hole in the cardstock so your **GIFT TAGS** can be easily attached to the Christmas gifts with a piece of string.

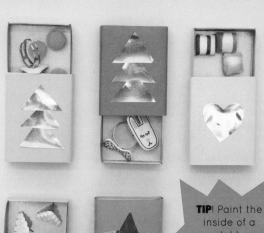

TIP! Paint the inside of a matchbox and cover the outside with pretty paper, and presto! You've made a perfect **GIFT BOX** for small Christmas gifts!

GREAT GIFT WRAPPERS

ANIMAL BOXES!

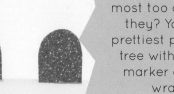

20

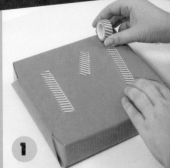

1. Wrap a gift in pretty paper.

2. Draw the eyes and mouth with a permanent marker.

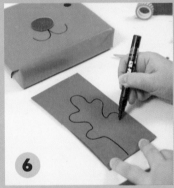

3. Draw a nose on another sheet of paper, using a round roll of tape as template, for example.

4. Cut out the nose with a pair of scissors.

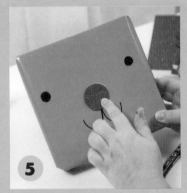

5. Glue the nose on, or attach it with some double-sided tape.

6. Draw reindeer horns or ears on a sheet of cardstock.

7. Cut them out with a pair of scissors.

8. Attach the ears to the package with some glue or double-sided tape. The reindeer is now ready!

GREAT GIFT WRAPPERS

Fun
CHRISTMAS CRAFTS

There are so many fun **CHRISTMAS CRAFTS** you can do. There a lot of old things you can use that you already have right at home! Plastic soda bottles, milk cartons, and empty toilet paper rolls are perfect to get us started!

22

1

To make a drinking straw star you'll need five drinking straws, a needle, and some string. Thread the needle with the string.

2

Cut off a long piece of thread—a little longer than the length of five drinking straws.

3

Start by threading all the drinking straws on to the string.

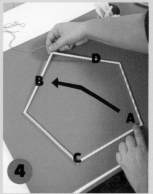

4

Make a knot at the very top, which will be the star's top. Lift corner A and put it against the left drinking straw, which is marked B in the picture.

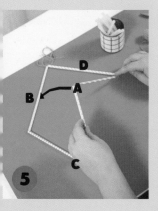

5

Place corner A across B's middle.

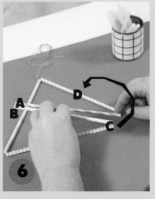

6

Two of the drinking straws are now lying against the left top drinking straw. Now lift C and place it against the center of the right drinking straw, which is marked D in the picture.

7

Look! You have made a star out of your five drinking straws.

8

At the points where the drinking straws connect with each other (where the fingers point to in the picture), secure them with some glue, tape, or string.

The **STRAW STARS** look great in the window or on a Christmas tree. You can hang the stars outside, too, if you use regular plastic straws.

FUN CHRISTMAS CRAFTS

Fill your new **ANIMAL BOTTLES** with candy, pens, a Christmas flower, or use them as a toothbrush holder.

TIP!

To remove the label: Just leave the bottle in some warm water for a little while, and the label will come straight off.

ANIMAL BOTTLES

HOW YOU DO IT

1. Start by removing the bottle's label and draw the shape of the animal on the bottle. Cut off the upper section of the bottle with scissors, and cut alongside the line that you've drawn (on the next page, you'll see the fun things you can make using the top part)!

2. Spray-paint the animal outside (lay down some protective covering, and be sure to use gloves and a mouth mask). You can also paint the animal with hobby paint and a brush.

3. Once the paint has dried, you can draw the eyes, mouth, and cheeks with a permanent marker.

4. Cut out a nose and glue it on.

YOU'LL NEED:

Spray paint (or hobby paint and a brush)

Protective covering
Mouth mask
Colored paper

Glue
Gloves
Plastic soda bottle

Permanent markers
Scissors

CANDY DISHES

HOW YOU DO IT

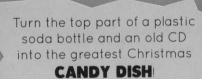

1. Cut off the top part of a plastic soda bottle with a pair of scissors (look on the previous page to see what fun things you can do with the bottom section).

2. Glue the bottle top (upside down) onto an old CD.

3. Spray paint the candy bowl outside (or paint it with hobby paint and a brush). Use protective covering, gloves, and a mouth mask. Let the bowl dry for about one hour.

4. Tie a ribbon around the bottom of the bowl, and now it's ready to be filled with candy!

YOU'LL NEED:

Spray paint (or hobby paint and a brush)
Protective covering
Mouth mask
Gloves
Old CDs

Glue
Scissors
Plastic soda bottle
Silk ribbon (or any other pretty ribbon)

Turn the top part of a plastic soda bottle and an old CD into the greatest Christmas **CANDY DISH**!

CAUTION!

Always use gloves and a mouth mask when using spray paint.

GINGERBREAD HOUSE TOWN

Save any empty milk cartons, rice boxes, potato chip cans, and other disposable packaging you find at home, and turn them into your very own **GINGERBREAD HOUSE TOWN**!

YOU'LL NEED:

Empty cartons
Hobby paint and brushes
Colored paper
Glue

Permanent markers
Scissors
Cotton

1 Paint a layer of white hobby paint on a milk carton.

2 When the white paint has dried, paint the carton with brown paint.

3 Cut out a piece of sturdy paper, big enough to make a roof.

4 Glue the roof paper onto the top of the carton, on the side without the opening.

5 Use the carton's cap as a template to draw the opening for the chimney on the roof paper.

6 Cut out the hole for the chimney with a pair of small scissors.

7 Glue the roof paper onto the side with the opening.

8 Cut off the sides of the roof if they are too long.

9 Cut a narrow piece of paper to make the chimney.

10 Measure how long it needs to be to go all around the chimney opening.

11 Put a dab of glue on one of the short ends on the narrow piece of paper.

12 Glue the narrow paper piece together to make a small tube.

13 Glue the paper tube onto the milk carton, around the chimney opening.

14 Fill the chimney opening with cotton balls.

15 Cut out doors and windows using the paper, and glue them on to the houses.

16 Paint the doors and windows. Do it again to make a whole town!

FUN CHRISTMAS CRAFTS

Use skewers and a variety of pretty paper to make cool masks and hats. They make great **PHOTO PROPS**!

PHOTO PROPS

HOW YOU DO IT

1. On the back of a sheet of cardstock, draw a triangle (which will become the hat) and a circle (which will become the top of the hat).

2. Cut out the triangle and the circle with a pair of scissors.

3. Glue the circle to the top of the hat, and attach a wooden skewer to the back of the hat with some glue or tape.

4. Make bow ties, eyeglasses, Santa hats, or anything that would be fun to use when you take Christmas selfies.

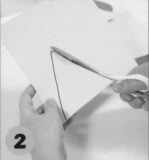

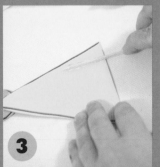

28

YOU'LL NEED:
Cardstock
Wooden skewers
Scissors
Glue or tape

WINTRY FOXES

HOW YOU DO IT

YOU'LL NEED:

Empty toilet paper roll
Hobby paint
Brush
Glue
Miniature pom-pom balls (find them at hobby stores)
Permanent markers
Pipe cleaners

1. Paint the toilet paper roll with white hobby paint. Let the paint dry.

2. Using another color, paint a triangle at the top of the roll and a half circle at the bottom.

3. Turn the roll so the back side faces you. Fold down the top like in the picture.

4. Do the same thing on the front side— now the fox has ears!

5. Draw the eyes and nose with a permanent marker.

6. Cut a pipe cleaner in half and glue a pompom ball to each end of the pipe cleaner to give the fox some earmuffs. Keep a finger on the earmuffs until the glue has set.

Use empty toilet paper rolls to make **WINTRY FOXES.** They make great decorations for the table or as Christmas tree ornaments.

FUN CHRISTMAS CRAFTS

CHRISTMAS PIÑATA

YOU'LL NEED:
Corrugated
cardboard
Scissors
Tape
Glue
Wrapping tissue
String
Black paper

Fill your **PIÑATA** with lots of great candy and invite your friends over for an after-Christmas party! Take turns beating the piñata with a stick until it bursts and all the treats fall out!

1

Cut out two Christmas trees—both pieces should be identical—and a few narrow strips of corrugated cardboard.

2

Bend the strips all along their length so they are easier to shape.

3

Fold and attach the strips with tape along the sides of one of the tree segments.

4

Punch a hole at the top of the tree with a pencil.

5

Pull a piece of thick string through the hole and tie the end around a match or a piece of drinking straw. That way the string stays firmly in place.

6

Fill the tree with lots of candy and confetti to make it extra festive when the piñata bursts!

7

Place the other tree segment on top (it becomes a lid) and attach it with tape all around.

8

Get out the wrapping tissue and cut fringes in long strips. Place several strips on top of each other while you cut to make the work go faster.

9

Attach the strips of tissue to the tree with a glue stick or other type of glue. Start from the bottom of the tree and work your way to the top.

10

You can cut the edges off the strips once the entire side of the tree is covered. Continue to attach strips to the edges and then the back of the tree.

11

When the entire tree is done, take some black paper and cut out eyes and a mouth.

12

Glue on the eyes and the mouth. Now, let's hang that piñata!

Excellent ORNAMENTS

Who needs store-bought ornaments? You can make the best **CHRISTMAS TREE ORNAMENTS** yourself! Paper, fuse beads, and candy are a huge hit on the tree!

PAPER PINE TREES

1. Copy the template of the tree that's on page 44. You'll learn how to trace it on that page, too.

2. Cut out the tree with a pair of scissors.

3. Make a hole at the top of the tree with a hole punch or a needle.

4. Tie some string through the hole, and hang the tree on your Christmas tree. You can hang it on its own, or make several paper trees and string them together like a garland.

CANDY GARLAND

Use a large needle and string to link together your **FAVORITE CANDY**, and hang candy garland on the Christmas tree!

EXCELLENT ORNAMENTS

Do you have a few small forgotten toys in a drawer somewhere? Give them new life as **KNICKKNACK CUPS**!

YOU'LL NEED:

Cardstock
Clear plastic cups
Ribbon or string
Permanent marker

A small toy
Glue
Scissors

KNICKKNACK CUPS

HOW YOU DO IT

1. Take a plastic cup and place it upside down on a sheet of cardstock. Use the cup as template and draw around the edge of the cup.

2. Now you have what will become the bottom of the cup. Attach a small toy or something fun to it with glue.

3. Apply glue all along the ring you just drew.

4. Press the plastic cup onto the glue circle and let the glue set for a little while.

5. Once the glue has dried, cut away the excess paper around the plastic cup.

6. Attach a nice ribbon or a piece of string at the top of the cup with a dot of glue. Let the glue dry for a few hours, and then hang the cup on the Christmas tree.

NOSY REINDEER

HOW YOU DO IT

1. Cut a pipe cleaner in half—and then cut those pieces in half so you end up with four pieces.

2. Fold and tie one piece of pipe cleaner around another one to make an antler. Do the same with the other two pieces of pipe cleaner.

3. Attach the antlers to the top of the Christmas tree ornament with a bit of glue, and keep holding them up against the ball until the glue dries. Use a glue gun if you have one—it dries in a flash.

4. Attach the eyes with a dot of glue. If you don't have any store-bought eyes, cut some paper into the shape of eyes, or draw them on with a permanent marker. Attach a pom-pom ball nose, or one made of paper, and let the glue dry.

HANG YOUR NOSY REINDEER ON THE CHRISTMAS TREE!

Find some old forgotten ornaments and turn them into **NOSY REINDEER!**

EXCELLENT ORNAMENTS

Use fuse beads to make some cool **CANDY GARLAND** to hang on the tree!

CANDY GARLAND

HOW YOU DO IT

1. Use fuse beads in a variety of colors and your fuse bead pegboard to make candy. You can find great patterns for this online.

2. Fuse the beads with an iron. Be sure to place some parchment paper between the beads and the iron. Ask a grown-up to help you if you haven't used an iron before.

3. Tie the candy to a piece of string.

4. Hang the garland in the Christmas tree.

YOU'LL NEED:

Iron
Parchment paper
String

Plastic fuse beads
Fuse bead pegboard

YARN POM-POMS

HOW YOU DO IT

1. Wind the yarn tightly around a fork. Make sure you don't get any yarn in the spaces between the tines.

2. When you've wound lots of yarn around the fork, poke a short piece of yarn through the middle space between the fork's tines.

3. With that short piece of yarn, make a tight double knot around the wound yarn.

4. Slide the ball of yarn off the fork, and cut open the sides of the ball with a pair of scissors. Tidy up and trim the strands of the ball until you have a nice round shape.

YOU'LL NEED:
Yarn
Scissors
Fork

Make small, quick and easy **POM-POMS** with a fork!

EXCELLENT ORNAMENTS

Sweet TREATS

Meringue trees on a stick and a candy-filled train made with bars of chocolate. It's time for Christmas's most wonderful **TREATS AND GOODIES**!

A **CANDY TRAIN** comes loaded!

YOU'LL NEED:

Chocolate bars
Stove and saucepan
Microwave
Freezer bag
Sharp knife
Candy and cookies

HOW YOU DO IT

1 Put the chocolate bars in the microwave for 30–60 seconds at full power. This makes them softer and easier to cut with a knife.

2 Carefully separate the chocolate bars using the template on page 45. Try to saw through the chocolate with the knife—that way the chocolate bar won't break so easily.

3 Melt a few pieces of chocolate over a water bath.

> Read at the bottom of the page how to make a **WATER BATH**. Look for me!

4 Pour the melted chocolate into a plastic freezer bag. Cut a small hole in one of the bag's corners.

5 Pipe the melted chocolate onto the wagons' edges. Use the chocolate as glue when you put together the train wagons. This is a bit tricky, but it's so much fun!

6 Put all pieces together following the instructions on page 45, and cover any mistakes with candy!

7 You can turn a marshmallow into a chimney. Attach it with some melted chocolate.

8 Use round candies or cookies for wheels. Attach them with melted chocolate, too.

9 Decorate the train with candy, and fill the wagons with enough Christmas candy to last you till New Year's Eve!

TIP!
You'll find the template for the wagons and the caboose on page 45.

How to make a **WATER BATH**:

1. Bring water to boil in a saucepan.

2. Place the chocolate in a deep plate, and place the plate on the saucepan like a lid.

3. Once the chocolate has melted, it's ready to be poured into the plastic freezer bag.

Be careful, because the steam from the water can be extremely hot. Ask a grown-up to help you if you haven't used the stove-top before.

SWEET TREATS

TIP!

Use white chocolate so it won't show against the marshmallow.

TIP!

Store the snowmen in plastic freezer bags to keep them nice for a few days.

SNOWMEN

HOW YOU DO IT

1. Slide three marshmallows onto a straw or a skewer. The easiest way to do this is to turn the straw or skewer like a screw through the marshmallow.

2. Break a straight pretzel stick in half and stick the pieces of pretzel into the middle marshmallow to make arms.

3. Put a few pieces of chocolate in the microwave for a few seconds so the chocolate starts melting.

4. Dip a pretzel stick into the melted chocolate, and use it to put dots on the front of the snowman to make candy buttons and eyes.

5. Make a hat out of a marshmallow and a cookie. Assemble the hat with some melted chocolate.

6. Attach the hat to the snowman, and he's ready to be eaten!

YOU'LL NEED:

Marshmallows
Straight pretzel sticks
Chocolate bar
Microwave
Drinking straws or wooden skewers
Mini chocolate buttons (such as mini M&Ms®)

40

1

2

3

4

5

6

CHOCOLATE BALLS

HOW YOU DO IT

1. Put 1 ¼ cup old-fashioned rolled oats, ½ cup granulated sugar, 3 tbsp cocoa, 1 tbsp vanilla sugar, and 7 tbsp butter into a bowl.

2. Mix all the ingredients thoroughly, and shape into balls as large as you want them to be.

3. Put candy canes in a plastic bag and crush them with a hammer (or use a mortar and pestle, if you have one at home). Put a cutting board under the bag so you don't damage the table.

4. Roll all the chocolate balls in the crushed candy cane, and put the balls in the refrigerator for half an hour before you serve them. Super simple and super yummy!

YOU'LL NEED:

Old-fashioned rolled oats	Vanilla sugar	Hammer or mortar and pestle
Granulated sugar	Butter	
Cocoa	Candy canes	Cutting board
	Plastic bag	

TIP!

Take an old chocolate box and cover it in pretty paper!

Merry Christmas!

merry xmas
feliz navidad
Bon
hyvää joulua
メリークリスマス
God Jul

MERINGUE CHRISTMAS TREES

YOU'LL NEED:

Large eggs
Granulate sugar
Vinegar
Piping bag or
freezer bag
Candy sprinkles
Paper drinking straws
or wooden skewers
Parchment paper
and oven

HOW YOU DO IT

1

Separate the whites from the yellows (yolks) of **two eggs**: Crack the eggshell and split it into two halves. Keep moving the yolk between the halves, making the whites run into a bowl underneath. Make sure NO yolk ends up in the bowl.

2

Set aside the bowl with the egg yolks, and put **one teaspoon of vinegar** in the bowl with the egg whites.

3

Pour ¼ **cup of granulated sugar** into the bowl.

4

With a handheld electric mixer, beat the egg whites, vinegar, and sugar until you have a firm batter.

5

When the batter is very firm, carefully add another ½ **cup granulated sugar** and beat it into the batter. If you want to, you can turn the batter green with some food coloring.

6

Pour the meringue batter into a piping bag, or into a plastic freezer bag in which you have snipped a large enough opening in one of the bottom corners.

7

Line a baking sheet with parchment paper. Pipe out a straight line of meringue onto the cookie sheet. Place a paper drinking straw or a wooden skewer along the line of meringue.

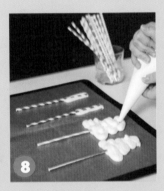

8

Pipe a pine tree onto the drinking straw or wooden skewer. Make the tree larger at the bottom, and narrower as you go toward the top.

9

Garnish the trees with candy sprinkles, and bake the trees in the oven at 225° F for 90 minutes. Let the trees cool—then go ahead and enjoy!

YUM!

SWEET TREATS

TEMPLATES

Templates for the **PAPER PINE TREES** on page 33

To **TRACE**, you'll put some thin paper (parchment paper, for example) over the template and draw the lines. Then cut out your template, place it on thicker paper, and draw along the edges.

Design for the **CANDY TRAIN** on page 38

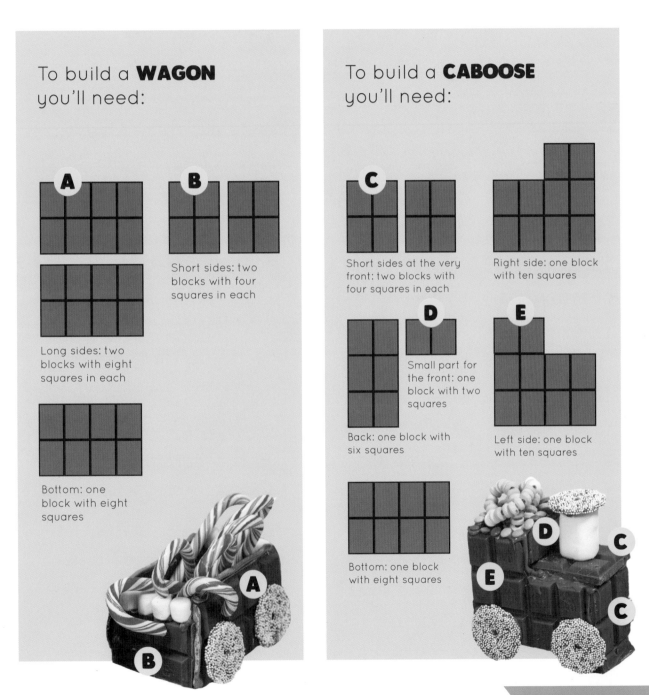

To build a **WAGON** you'll need:

A

Long sides: two blocks with eight squares in each

B

Short sides: two blocks with four squares in each

Bottom: one block with eight squares

To build a **CABOOSE** you'll need:

C

Short sides at the very front: two blocks with four squares in each

Right side: one block with ten squares

D

Small part for the front: one block with two squares

Back: one block with six squares

E

Left side: one block with ten squares

Bottom: one block with eight squares

TEMPLATES